COLLECTAFACT™

WORDS AND PICTURES ⟩ THAT WORK TOGETHER

ANCIENT GREECE

LONDON · PRINCETON

What's in the book

4 The Greek world
Where did the ancient
Greeks live?

6 Land and climate
What were the lands of
ancient Greece like?

8 The five ages of
ancient Greece
Discover how the Greeks
changed over time

10 The city states
Looking at Greek cities
and territories

12 A divided Greece
Learn about the battles
that waged in ancient times

14 Citizens and slaves
Find out about the power
of the Greek people

16 Philosophy and
science
The great thinkers and
their key discoveries

18 Gods and
goddesses
Believing in mythology,
soothsayers and oracles

20 Theatre and writing
What the ancient Greeks
did for entertainment

22 At home
Inside a typical ancient
Greek house

*All words in the text which appear in **bold** can be found in the glossary*

24 **Food**
What did the ancient Greeks eat and drink?

26 **Arts and crafts**
Some classic examples of the Greek style!

28 **Language and learning**
Did the Greeks go to school?

29 **The legend of the Minotaur**
A traditional Greek story

34 **How we know**
The evidence that's been left behind

35 **Glossary**
Key words explained in detail

38 **Activities**
Note pages for your own use plus a chance to be creative!

44 **Questions and answers**
All your Greek questions answered

46 **Index**
An easy way to find topics of interest

ITALY

Adriatic Sea

Pindus Mountains

MACEDONIA

TROY

Aegean Sea

Delphi

Athens

Ionian Sea

Olympia

Peloponnese

Sparta

Sea of Crete

CRETE
Home of
the Minotaur

The Greek world

The civilisation of ancient Greece began around 2000 BC. The Greeks controlled the mainland and the islands we now know as Greece. As the civilisation expanded, traders and farmers settled in the lands at the eastern end of the Mediterranean Sea.

The peak of the Greek civilisation was known as the **Classical period**, between 479 BC and 323 BC. During this time, the Greeks developed many new ideas about science and the arts. Some of their ideas and inventions influenced other civilisations in Europe at that time. From there, Greek ideas spread all around the world.

ASIA MINOR

Land conquered by **Alexander the Great**

RHODES

CYPRUS

The Greeks travelled to these areas to farm the land.

Mediterranean Sea

FastFact
One of the ancient battle tactics was to row very fast towards a ship and ram into the side of it!

Alexandria

EGYPT

Land and climate

Mainland Greece and the nearby islands are hot and dry, with high mountains and steep-sided valleys. The mainland is surrounded almost entirely by water. It was once covered in forest but, by the **Classical period**, many trees had been cut down. The scarce farmland was located mainly near the coast, or in sheltered valleys.

The most important crops were wheat, barley, grapes and olives. The Greeks were skilled sailors and keen traders, and they imported a lot of their food from other countries. There were few good roads and most journeys had to be made on foot. Some village communities were very isolated.

▼ As travelling overland was so difficult, the Greeks often travelled by sea. They found their way by staying close to the coasts. The sea was often stormy and sometimes there were attacks by pirates.

▶ This picture shows some olive trees growing on a dry, rocky hillside.

FastFact
In Delphi, there was a stone called the Omphalos that the Greeks believed marked the centre of the Earth.

The five ages of ancient Greece

People have been living in the lands of Greece for over 40,000 years! The early Greek people lived in caves. Instead of farming their food, they hunted animals and gathered plants to eat.

Around 6500 BC, the Greek way of life was just beginning. Small groups of people lived on the islands in the Aegean Sea and the Sea of Crete. The people in this region grew crops, kept sheep and made clay pots. Most of their tools and weapons were made from stone.

In the strong and influential ancient Greek civilisation that grew from these groups of people, there were five major periods of time.

The Bronze Age: 3000–1000 BC

The Bronze Age was when the Greeks began to use **bronze** to make their crafts, tools and weapons. Around 1900 BC, there were two main groups of people living in ancient Greece. The Minoans lived on the island of Crete, and the Myceneans lived on the mainland of Greece.

In 1500 BC, a huge volcano erupted near Crete and many Minoan people were killed. Soon after, their capital city, Knossos, burned down and was never rebuilt. In 1250 BC, the Trojan War began. It lasted ten years.

The Dark Age: 1000–800 BC

The ancient Greeks have kept us in the dark about this period! There are no written records from this time because, in the Dark Age, hardly anyone knew how to read and write. Instead, people kept their legends alive with traditional songs and stories.

We do know that the population of Greece became smaller around this time. By the time of the Dark Age in ancient Greece, the powerful Egyptian civilisation had come to an end. In China, the Shang Dynasty was also ending.

The Archaic period: 800–479 BC

During the Archaic period, the Greek civilisation began to spread to other lands around the Mediterranean Sea, and the **city states** began to form.

Until about 800 BC, the Greeks had not used writing for hundreds of years. During the Archaic period, the Greeks began to write again. **Homer** is thought to have composed his two famous poems about the Trojan War around this time: *The Iliad* and *The Odyssey*.

In 776 BC, the first ever Olympic Games were held at Olympia.

The Classical period: 479–323 BC

The ancient Greek civilisation reached its peak during the Classical period. Part of this period, from about 477 BC onwards, is known as the Golden Age. The arts, such as plays, stories, **sculpture** and architecture, flourished. The discoveries and teachings of the **philosophers** of this time continue to influence people today.

In 431 BC, the Peloponnesian war broke out between Athens and Sparta. After 27 years, Athens was conquered. In 338 BC, Greece was defeated in a war against Macedonia and, by 323 BC, Greek independence had ended.

The Hellenistic Age: 323–31 BC

In 323 BC, **Alexander the Great** died. The period after his death is known as the Hellenistic Age. For the next 150 years, Greece was ruled by the Macedonians.

During the Hellenistic Age, another empire was growing not far away. By 272 BC, the Romans had conquered most of Italy. Around 146 BC, the Romans conquered Greece and Macedonia. The Roman Empire was large and powerful but this did not destroy the Greek way of life. In fact, many Greek traditions became part of the Roman way of life.

The city states

Greece was not always the united country that it is today. It was once made up of separate **city states**. Each city state was based around one city and included the surrounding farms and villages.

Athens was one of the largest and most powerful city states. At the height of the **Classical period**, there were more than 250,000 people living in the city and the surrounding countryside. Artists, **philosophers** and politicians from Athens were famous throughout Greece.

▼ This is the ancient city of Athens. On a hill, called the Acropolis, was the Parthenon, the main temple of the city. In the centre of town was the busy agora, where markets took place.

FastFact
The ancient Greek tradition of the Olympic Games has continued until today. In AD 393, however, a Roman emperor banned the games.

Athens versus Sparta

Sparta was Athens' main rival. There were many wars between the two cities as they both tried to gain control of the whole of Greece. Sparta was famed for the strength of its army. In 431 BC, the rivalry between the two cities led to the Peloponnesian War. After 27 years of fighting, Sparta won the war.

▲ This vase painting shows some Greek soldiers in battle.

▶ Ancient Greek soldiers used weapons and armour made from iron or bronze.

A divided Greece

Life was not always peaceful in ancient Greece. The people lived in many different **city states**. Some of these were friends but others were enemies.

Over the course of hundreds of years, there were many wars between the city states. There were also independent territories, which did not get involved in the fighting at all, and some pirates.

The two worst enemies were Sparta and Athens. By 500 BC, they were the most powerful city states and they each had many **allies**.

Corinth

Corinth helped to start the Peloponnesian War. In 431 BC, Corinth had a disagreement with Corcyra. Corcyra is an island to the west of Greece, in the Ionian Sea. Today, it is called Corfu. The disagreement escalated into a battle and the two biggest city states, Sparta and Athens, had to step in with extra troops. Sparta backed Corinth, while Athens supported Corcyra. This led to the Peloponnesian war.

The Spartan allies

Sparta had the finest army of all the city states. To the Spartans, war was the most important part of life. All Spartan men were expected to join the army. Boys trained as soldiers when they were only seven years old! Sparta and Athens both wanted to control Greece. The Peloponnesian war between Athens and Sparta started in 431 BC. Sparta eventually defeated Athens after 27 years of fighting, and ruled over Greece. But the Spartans were not as good at ruling as they were at fighting. They only stayed in power for about 30 years before they were defeated by the Thebans.

The Thebans

The warriors of Thebes were the most hated in Greece. This was probably because they were always changing their mind about which side they were on! Firstly, the Thebans joined the Persians. Then they became allies with Sparta but later turned against them. And the next time there was a war against the Persians, the Thebans stayed on the Greek side! Eventually, Thebes was destroyed by **Alexander the Great**'s armies.

The Persian Empire

In 550 BC, the Persian **Empire** began to expand and soon ruled over parts of Asia Minor and Egypt. The Persians conquered the Greek territories in the west of Asia Minor. In 499 BC, the Greeks rebelled, and over the next 20 years they won a series of wars against the Persians. In 359 BC, Philip II became king of Macedonia. His armies were strong and, in 338 BC, Greece fell under Macedonian control. Two years later, Philip died and his son Alexander became king. Alexander was a brilliant soldier and in 324 BC, with an army of 35,000 men, he conquered the whole of the Persian Empire.

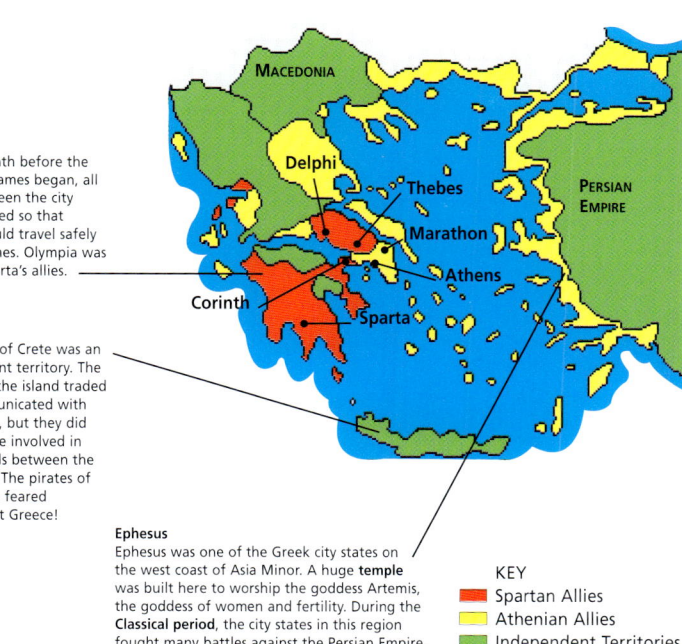

Olympia
In the month before the Olympic Games began, all wars between the city states ceased so that people could travel safely to the games. Olympia was one of Sparta's allies.

Crete
The island of Crete was an independent territory. The people of the island traded and communicated with the Greeks, but they did not become involved in the quarrels between the city states. The pirates of Crete were feared throughout Greece!

Ephesus
Ephesus was one of the Greek city states on the west coast of Asia Minor. A huge **temple** was built here to worship the goddess Artemis, the goddess of women and fertility. During the **Classical period**, the city states in this region fought many battles against the Persian Empire.

MACEDONIA

Delphi

Thebes

Marathon

Athens

Corinth

Sparta

PERSIAN EMPIRE

KEY
🟥 Spartan Allies
🟨 Athenian Allies
🟩 Independent Territories

The Athenian allies

Athens was the greatest of the city states. It was here that the ancient Greek civilisation reached its peak. The Athenians were successful in battle, too. They had a large fleet of ships, called **triremes**, and many allies around the Aegean Sea. But on land, the Athenian army was not so strong. Unlike many other city states, Athens did not have a permanent army. Instead, all men between the ages of 20 and 50 were on call to go into battle when war broke out. They suffered heavily in some of the land-based battles against enemies such as Sparta and Macedonia.

Citizens and slaves

In ancient Greece, some groups of people had different rights from others. **Citizens** were the most important group of people and they had the most rights. They could own property and take part in **politics**. Only adult men were allowed to be citizens in ancient Greece.

Slaves were the property of their owners and they had no rights at all. Many slaves lived in miserable conditions. But some slaves were paid for the work that they did and, if they saved enough money, they could buy their freedom.

▲ These are some ancient Greek coins.

▼ Soldiers often watched over slaves as they worked.

FastFact
In the late 19th century, the remains of the original games' stadium at Olympia were found. In 1896, the first modern Olympics were held in Athens.

Government

In many of the **city states** in ancient Greece, the government was run as a **democracy**. All of the decisions about the city state were made by councils of citizens. Other city states, however, were ruled by rich and powerful landowners.

In Athens, all citizens could vote to decide on issues such as the type of taxes to be paid and whether or not to go to war. All citizens could take part in politics and legal affairs. Some citizens were paid a full day's wages to attend the government assemblies.

▲ This vase painting shows some women collecting water. Women didn't have the same rights as men in ancient Greece.

▲ Discs such as these were used to vote in courts of law. Hollow discs stood for 'guilty' and solid discs stood for 'not guilty'.

▲ Citizens could vote against a politician by writing his name on a pottery fragment, called an ostrakon.

Philosophy and science

The ancient Greeks were curious about themselves and the world around them. They made many important advances in science, learning and the arts. Great thinkers were known as **philosophers**, no matter what subject they studied. The word philosopher comes from the Greek words for 'lover of wisdom'. Philosophers tried to find out how the universe worked and how people should best live their lives.

Many Greek discoveries provide the foundations of our knowledge and beliefs.

The Greeks studied the stars and learned that the Earth floats freely in space and turns on an imaginary line, called an axis. They also correctly predicted eclipses of the Sun. But sometimes the Greeks were wrong. One scholar, called Ptolemy, thought that the Earth was the centre of the universe.

Few of the Greeks' ideas were used for solving practical problems. For example, they did not use their metal-working techniques to make tools that would increase their knowledge of science.

Famous philosophers

● **Socrates (about 469–399 BC)**
Socrates was one of the first great philosophers of Classical Greece. He questioned many of the beliefs of the time.

● **Hippocrates (about 469–399 BC)**
Hippocrates was alive at the same time as Socrates. He practised scientific medicine and studied the human body.

● **Plato (about 429–347 BC)**
Plato founded a school in Athens, called The Academy, where he taught Aristotle.

● **Aristotle (about 384–322 BC)**
Aristotle examined things in nature and developed a way of thinking called logic.

▲ A bust of Socrates.

◄ The philosopher Eratosthenes used the Sun to calculate the circumference of the Earth. At noon, the Sun was directly overhead in Syene, in Southern Egypt. So, he measured the angle of the Sun at Alexandria, in Northern Egypt, and then measured the distance between the two places. His calculation of the Earth's circumference was out by just 320km.

FastFact
In Spartan schools, boys were taught to be tough. They had to sleep on the ground and were beaten if they misbehaved.

Gods and goddesses

The Greeks worshipped many gods and goddesses that represented parts of human life or the natural world. The gods were thought to live on **Mount Olympus** and there were many stories about them, in which they fought amongst each other or fell in love, just like men and women.

There were many **temples** where **priests** or **priestesses** performed rituals in honour of the gods. Offerings of food and wine were made and, sometimes during **festivals**, **sacrifices** were made.

The Greeks believed that the gods controlled events. So they looked to the gods for answers to their problems. Some problems were solved by a **soothsayer**, who studied the weather, or the remains of animals, for answers from the gods. Other problems required a visit to an **oracle**, where a priest or priestess passed on messages from the gods.

▼ At the oracle in Delphi, a priestess, called the Pythia, went into a trance to receive messages from the gods.

The Olympic Games

In ancient Greece, games and festivals were held to honour the gods. The Olympic Games were held in Olympia in honour of Zeus every four years. They lasted for five days, and the events included boxing, wrestling, running, long-jump, discus-throwing, javelin-throwing and chariot races. People came from all over Greece to compete in the games. All wars were postponed so that people could travel safely to see them.

Important gods

Zeus was the king of the gods.
Hera was married to Zeus and was the queen of the gods.
Poseidon was the god of the sea.
Dionysus was the god of wine.
Ares was the god of war.
Hermes was the messenger of the gods.
Apollo was the god of music and healing.

▲ Aphrodite, the goddess of love.

◄ Athena, the goddess of wisdom, was born from the head of Zeus.

Theatre and writing

The ancient Greeks were one of the first groups of people to record their **history** as it happened. Before this, people had passed on information by word of mouth.

Poetry was the earliest form of Greek literature. Many of the Greek poems told stories about heroes and gods. **Homer** was an ancient storyteller. He composed two **epic** poems, called *The Iliad* and *The Odyssey*. These and many other examples of Greek literature have survived until today.

▲ The actors in comedies wore padded costumes to make them look funny.

Drama

Drama developed from songs and dances that honoured the gods. Plays were an important part of religious **festivals** and many of the theatres were built next to temples. There were two sorts of plays: tragedies and comedies. Comedies made fun of **politics**, religion and important people. Tragedies were sad tales about gods, heroes and legendary people.

▶ Greek actors always wore masks that showed different moods and expressions. The masks had wide mouths so that the actors' voices could be heard.

FastFact
Today, more than three million people live in Athens. Many of the ancient buildings are still standing.

At home

In ancient Greece, ordinary people lived in simple houses that were made from mud bricks. It was so easy to dig through the walls that burglars were known as wall-diggers! Each house was arranged around a courtyard, with an altar in the middle. The living rooms were on the ground floor, with bedrooms above.

Men and women often had separate living areas and spent most of their time apart. There were open fires in the kitchen and smoke escaped through a hole in the roof.

▼ This is the inside of a typical ancient Greek house.

kitchen

altar

living room

herm

Clothes

Men in ancient Greece wore tunics made from wool or linen. Over this, they wore a square piece of material, called a **chiton**, fastened at the shoulders and belted at the waist. In colder weather, men wore a cloak, called a **himation**, draped around them. In Classical times, it was very fashionable for men to have beards.

Women wore a long tunic, called a **peplos**. Wealthy people wore tunics made from decorated material, while slaves had plain tunics. Shoes were leather sandals or boots but many people went barefoot.

▼ A gold necklace of the sort worn by the woman in the vase painting (bottom).

bathroom

well

► This vase painting shows a woman getting ready for her wedding. She is wearing a peplos.

◄ Some houses had a statue of the god Hermes, called a herm, to guard the house.

Food

The ancient Greeks had a simple and healthy diet. They ate bread, cheese, vegetables, fruit, eggs and meat. Many Greeks lived near the sea, so fish and seafood were popular. Olive oil was used for cooking, lighting and cleaning.

The main meal was in the evening and the Greeks often held big dinner parties. They sat on couches, eating several courses and drinking lots of wine. After the meal, there was entertainment for the men at a **symposium**, or drinking party.

▲ This vase painting shows a messenger of the gods bringing a gift of grain.

> **FastFact**
> As the Greek civilisation expanded, the Roman empire was just beginning. The city of Rome was founded in about 753 BC.

▼ These are some examples of fruit that the ancient Greeks liked to eat.

pomegranates

figs

olives

dried dates

fresh dates

Greek sweetmeats

Between courses at a dinner party, the Greeks ate sweetmeats – small snacks made from dates, figs, nuts, sesame seeds and honey.

Here are some for you to make. Put 100g of sesame seeds into a saucepan with 4 large tablespoons of honey. Ask an adult to help you simmer the mixture over a low heat for 10–20 minutes, until it is a rich, golden colour. You can tell if it is ready by dropping a spoonful on to a wet plate, letting it cool, then working it into a ball. If it keeps its shape, it is ready. Take the pan off the heat and stir the mixture every few minutes until it is almost cold. Wet your hands with cold water and roll spoonfuls of the mixture into 20–25 little balls. Wrap each sweetmeat in greaseproof paper.

grapes

Arts and crafts

The Greeks thought that there was a perfect shape for every object, whether it was a simple clay pot or a huge **temple**. They used mathematics to try to make their art as beautiful as possible.

▲ The Greeks made elegant pots covered in patterns and paintings. Most of the pots were used every day, for storing water, oil, or wine. Some of the most beautiful pots were buried with the dead.

◀ This statue is made from stone. The ancient Greeks were skilled sculptors and they made many statues from stone or bronze. The statues were detailed and lifelike, with expressive faces and clothes that looked real. Many of them were painted but have lost their colour over time.

▶ The Parthenon can still be found in Athens. It is one of the finest examples of ancient Greek architecture that is standing today. It was made from carved blocks of cream-coloured marble, held together with wooden pegs and metal clamps. The rows of columns are typical of ancient Greek buildings. This Classical style has been copied all over the world.

Bronze statues

Bronze statues were made using the 'lost wax' method.

▼ When the clay and pegs were finally removed, a bronze statue was revealed.

Firstly, a clay model was made and strengthened with wooden pegs. Then, the model was covered with a thin layer of wax. Next, the details of the statue, such as the face and clothes, were sculpted onto the wax.

The model was then covered with clay and heated, so the wax melted and ran out. Molten bronze was poured in between the clay layers.

Language and learning

In ancient Greece, most children went to school. Boys went to school from the age of seven until they were 15, and learned reading, writing and maths, as well as music, poetry and sport. Some Greek girls learned reading, writing, gymnastics and music. Girls were also taught the skills that they would need to run a household.

In Sparta, boys were taught to be tough in order to prepare them for their life as soldiers. At the age of seven, they went to a strict school where they learned how to fight and use weapons. They often went hungry and had to sleep on the ground, and sometimes they were beaten.

▶ This ancient terracotta doll has jointed arms and legs.

◀ This is an ancient baby's bottle.

The Greek alphabet

Some Greek letters are similar to those we use today. You may have heard some of their names before. Can you think where the word 'alphabet' came from?

Greek letter	Name	English sound		Greek letter	Name	English sound		Greek letter	Name	English sound		Greek letter	Name	English sound
A α	alpha	a		H η	eta	ey		N ν	nu	n		T τ	tau	t
B β	beta	b		Θ θ	theta	th		Ξ ξ	xi	ks		Υ υ	upsilon	u
Γ γ	gamma	g		I ι	iota	i		O o	omicron	o		Φ φ	phi	ph
Δ δ	delta	d		K κ	kappa	k		Π π	pi	p		X χ	chi	ch
E ε	epsilon	e		Λ λ	lambda	l		P ρ	rho	r		Ψ ψ	psi	ps
Z ζ	zeta	z		M μ	mu	m		Σ σ,ς	sigma	s		Ω ω	omega	oh

The legend of the Minotaur

The ancient Greeks told myths about their gods and about the world around them. Myths often included real events from Greek history. This myth is about an early civilisation on the island of Crete, long before Athens was a powerful city state. It tells the story of Theseus, a heroic young man who overcame the Minotaur, a terrifying beast that was half-man and half-bull.

Athenians were afraid of the island of Crete and trembled at the mention of it. Every nine years, King Minos of Crete demanded a terrible tribute from the Athenians. Seven young men and seven young women were taken from Athens to be fed to the fearsome Minotaur.

King Minos would send a ship with black sails to Athens when the tribute was due. A huge crowd would gather at the harbour, weeping and wailing as the ship sailed away towards Crete.

When the prisoners arrived in Crete, they were given fine clothes and made guests of honour at a huge banquet. They were offered the most delicious food available, but they could hardly eat. Afterwards, they were shut in a luxurious room, but few of them could sleep.

The next day, they were taken to some huge, wooden doors, carved with pictures of galloping bulls. From behind the doors came the sounds of loud bellowing and stamping. The prisoners were very afraid.

Then, a guard opened the doors and pushed a prisoner through. The small crowd of prisoners, guards and priestesses outside heard a blood-curdling scream. A priestess pointed at the next prisoner to be sent through. This went on until all the prisoners had met their fate. Afterwards, the Athenians rested easy for nine years, until it was time to make another tribute.

Nine years passed and the dreaded ship was sent to Athens again. Amongst the prisoners sent to Crete this time was a young man, named Theseus. Unlike all the other prisoners, he sat dry-eyed on the ship. He laughed and chatted as they prepared for the banquet, which cheered up the other prisoners. At the banquet, Theseus sat next to King Minos' daughter, Ariadne, who was charmed by his courage and handsome looks.

Ariadne told Theseus that behind the doors there was an elaborate maze. The paths twisted and turned, confusing the eye and the mind. No-one who had entered the maze had ever returned.

The Minotaur lived at the heart of the maze. He knew all the twists, turns and blind alleys. If someone stumbled into the maze, the Minotaur could find him or her in moments.

Ariadne was determined to help Theseus. After the banquet, she crept into the sleeping chamber and called softly to him. All of Theseus' weapons had been taken away, so Ariadne handed him a sword. Then she led the way to the great carved wooden doors of the maze.

"I will wait here for you," she said and handed Theseus a ball of thread.

"What is this for?" Theseus said, puzzled. "As you walk through the maze, unwind this thread behind you. If you succeed, you can follow the thread back. The Minotaur will be asleep, so creep silently through the passages until you reach his lair. With surprise on your side, you may beat him," Ariadne replied.

Theseus took the thread from Ariadne and pushed open the great door. He stepped inside and closed the door, trapping the end of the thread in it. Then, holding his sword in front of him, Theseus headed into the maze.

Theseus could hear the Minotaur snoring and he headed towards the noise. But a few minutes later, he could no longer hear the snores. The path had doubled back, and Theseus was further away from the centre of the maze than when he had started. Theseus picked up the thread and followed it back to the last place where he had chosen a path.

"If I take the path that leads to the sounds, I end up further away," he said to himself. "Perhaps if I choose the path that seems to lead away, I will get closer to him."

Theseus crept quietly along and soon found himself stumbling into the mouth of

a dark cave. From inside, he heard a huge roar, followed by the sound of heavy footsteps. The Minotaur had woken up! Theseus gasped and dropped his sword.

The Minotaur was even more terrifying than he had imagined. It had the body of a huge man and the head of an angry bull. Just as the Minotaur leapt forward to grab him, Theseus picked up his sword and struck the Minotaur a terrible blow on the leg.

The Minotaur was in agony. He was not used to people fighting back – his victims were usually prisoners who did not resist. Theseus struck once more with his sword. The Minotaur was caught off guard – in a moment he lay dead at Theseus' feet!

Picking up the end of the thread, brave Theseus retraced his steps through the maze. Ariadne was waiting for him at the outer doors.

Theseus was proclaimed a hero by the people of Athens. They were overjoyed that Athens no longer had to pay such a terrible tribute to King Minos of Crete.

How we know

How do we know so much about the Greeks when they lived so long ago?

Evidence from the ground

The Greeks built many buildings and made many beautiful objects. Some of these were buried and **archaeologists** have been able to dig them up to learn from them. Pictures on pottery, for example, tell us about the way that people looked.

▲ The painting on this plate shows two Greek heroes fighting over the body of a soldier.

▲ This picture is from Roman times. It shows Alexander the Great, a famous Greek military leader, going into battle against the Persian Empire.

Evidence from books

The ancient Greeks were one of the first groups of people to keep written records. They wrote down all sorts of things, from **history** and **philosophy**, to lists of goods in stores. Some of these records have survived until today. They give us important clues about the ancient Greek way of life.

Evidence from around us

Greek buildings that remain standing today give us evidence of how the ancient Greeks lived. And some Greek words have become part of other European languages – especially words connected with science, such as 'psychology' and 'astronomy'.

▲ Theseus' temple still stands in Athens.

Glossary

Acropolis The hill within the boundary of a city state that was used for defence. This is a Greek word, meaning 'high city'.

agora An open area in the centre of ancient Greek cities where markets took place.

Alexander the Great The king of Macedonia and Greece who conquered the Persian Empire.

allies United territories.

archaeologist Someone who studies human history by uncovering ancient objects and physical remains.

Archaic period A period in history around 800–479 BC.

Ariadne Daughter of King Minos, who helped Theseus.

Aristotle A famous Greek philosopher, student of Plato. Aristotle died in 322 BC.

armour A covering, usually of metal, worn to protect the body when fighting.

BC Before Christ; the number of years before the year zero in the Western calendar.

bronze A metal that is made of copper, tin, zinc and lead.

Bronze Age A period in history around 3000–1000 BC.

chiton A garment Greek men wore fastened at the shoulders and belted around the waist.

citizen In ancient Greece, a citizen was a man who had the right to own property and take part in politics and the law.

city state An area of land around a Greek city, which had its own government but was considered a part of Greece. There were many city states in ancient Greece.

Classical period A period in history around 479–323 BC.

column A tall pillar, usually round, often supporting an arch or roof.

Dark Age A period in history around 1000–800 BC.

democracy A political system whereby citizens can vote for their chosen leaders and in doing so can influence decisions about the way their city or country is run.

dynasty A family that rules a country or empire for many generations.

empire A large group of states or countries ruled by a single government, usually an emperor.

epic A long, traditional poem that tells a story about heroes or the gods.

festival A special day, or several days, of celebration.

Helen of Troy Wife of the king of Sparta, Menelaus, and cause of the Trojan War.

Hellenistic Age A period in history around 323–31 BC.

himation A type of cloak worn by Greek men.

history The study of important or public events from the past.

Homer An ancient Greek storyteller Homer wrote two famous epic poems about the Trojan War. They are called *The Iliad* and *The Odyssey*.

knucklebones The bones from the ankles of animals,

such as pigs and goats, which were thrown into the air like dice.

logic A method of thinking a problem through carefully to find a solution.

Menelaus The king of Sparta, married to Helen of Troy.

Minos The king of Crete.

Minotaur A beast in Greek mythology who was half-man and half-bull. The Minotaur lived at the centre of a huge maze on the island of Crete.

monarchy A country that has a monarchy is ruled by a king or queen. Usually, when the king or queen dies, their son or daughter becomes the next ruler.

Mount Olympus The mountain in Greece where the gods were thought to live.

myths Traditional stories about gods or heroes. Greek mythology continues to influence writers today.

oracle A holy place where priests and priestesses asked the gods for advice.

ostrakon A pottery fragment that citizens wrote on to vote against a politician.

peplos A long tunic worn by women in ancient Greece.

philosopher A person who studies the world around them. This word comes from the Greek words for 'lover of wisdom'.

Plato A Greek philosopher who died in 347 BC.

politics This word, which comes from the Greek word, *politikos*, refers to the management of a country or state. A country's 'political system' is its rules of government.

priest A man who devotes his life to serving a god or gods.

priestess A woman who devotes her life to serving a god or gods.

sacrifice An offering, usually of an animal, made to the gods, asking them to bring good fortune to people.

sculpture Art in a solid form, such as a statue or carving. Sculpture was highly prized in ancient Greece.

slave A worker who was legally owned by a citizen in ancient Greece and had no rights at all. Slavery is now illegal in all countries.

soothsayer A person who could predict the future and tell fortunes.

Socrates One of the first Greek philosophers, Socrates lived in Athens from around 469 to 399 BC.

statue A model of a person, an animal or a god. Greek sculptors made many statues.

symposium A drinking party, attended by ancient Greek men, where entertainment took place.

temple A building for the worship of a god or goddess, or that is thought of as his or her home.

terracotta Brownish-red pottery used in building and modelling. The word comes from the Italian words for 'baked earth'.

Theseus A hero in Greek mythology who killed the Minotaur and ended the Athenians' nine-yearly human sacrifice to Crete.

tribute A gift that is given to show respect for someone.

triremes The biggest ships in the Athenian fleet. They were about 40m long and could reach speeds of up to 16km/h.

Work book

Photocopy this sheet and use it to make your own notes.

Photocopy this sheet and use it to make your own notes.

Draw your own Greek city

Questions and answers

The Pythia was the **priestess** at the **oracle** in Delphi in ancient Greece. She was very wise and people often went to ask her questions. She can answer all your questions about ancient Greek civilisation.

What did the Greeks discover about maths and science?

The ancient Greeks made many important discoveries in mathematics and science. For example, the scientist Democritus developed a theory that everything on Earth was made up of tiny particles, called atoms. This theory has been a key part of science since this important discovery.

The **temple** of the **priest** Trophonius was unusual in that only men were allowed to speak the words of the oracle. The cave in which Trophonius' oracle was found was said to be so awe-inspiring that people who entered and consulted the oracle never smiled again!

Priest

What did the Greeks discover about medicine?

Many people believed that illness was actually a punishment from the gods. But a **philosopher** called Hippocrates developed a scientific approach to medicine. He carefully studied the human body and performed experiments to discover the real causes of illness. Sometimes, Hippocrates is called the 'Father of Medicine'.

What was life like for women in ancient Greece?

Women in ancient Greece were not allowed to vote. They could go out to religious **festivals** or to visit friends, but they were expected to be accompanied by a friend or a **slave**. Women organised the household and the slaves, and spinning and weaving took up a lot of their time.

What was life like for children in ancient Greece?

At about seven years old children began to learn reading, writing, poetry, mathematics and music. But Greek children also played with dolls, rattles, dice or **knucklebones**, and even yo-yos.

How did the Greeks travel?

Wealthy people owned horses. Some merchants used carts, drawn by oxen or mules, to transport their goods. Most Greeks travelled on foot. Many people of the **city states** travelled in ships to trade.

What is a democracy?
A democracy is a system of government in which the leaders are chosen by the people. In ancient Greece, many of the city states were governed by a democracy. **Citizens** were able to vote, and could also become politicians and serve as members on juries in the law courts.

Who was Socrates?
Socrates was a philosopher who was sentenced to death by the citizens of Athens. They thought that he was a bad influence on young people and that he had tried to introduce new gods. Socrates' teachings and the story of his death were written down by another Greek philosopher, **Plato**.

What did the Greeks do in their spare time?
Most of the entertainment was based on religion. There were drama, poetry and music festivals to honour the gods. During the drama festivals, businesses closed and prisoners were allowed out of jail! Poetry was recited at festivals and private parties and often accompanied by music.

What is a marathon?
Marathon was a town in ancient Greece north-east of Athens. In 490 BC, the Persians landed here to attack the Athenians. An Athenian messenger was sent to Sparta to ask for help – and he ran all the way. That's about 240km! And that's why a long running race is called a marathon!

In ancient Greece, priestesses had a much easier life than other women. Women could not vote, and girls were given much less education than boys. The Pythia at Delphi was the priestess of Apollo. She got her inspiration for oracles by inhaling gases coming up from a hole in the ground, while sitting over it on a three-legged stool!

Priestess

Why were sports and athletics so important to the Greeks?
The Greeks believed that having a fit body was a way of honouring the gods, and they used sport as a way of training for warfare. Men's events included running, wrestling, boxing and javelin-throwing. In all of these events, the athletes competed naked! Women competed in running races. Greeks took the games very seriously, and breaking the rules in sport was punished severely.

FastFact
The Persian **Empire** was also expanding around 550 BC. The Persians become powerful at this time under the rule of a man named Cyrus the Great.

Index

A

Acropolis 10
agora 10
Alexander the Great 5, 12, 34
alphabet 28
Aristotle 17
arts 9, 16, 26–27, 34
Athens 4, 9, 10–11, 15, 17, 27, 29, 34

B

bronze 11, 26, 27
buildings 10, 22–23, 27, 34

C

children 28, 44

A (chiton etc.)

chiton 23
citizens 14–15
city states 10–11, 12–13, 15, 44
Classical period 4, 6, 10, 17, 23, 27
climate 6
clothes 23
crafts 26–27

D

democracy 15, 45
drama 9, 20–21

E

education 28
epic poem 20
Eratosthenes 17

F

farming 6
food 24–25

G

gods and goddesses 18–19
government 15, 45

H

herm 22, 23

himation 23
Hippocrates 17, 44
Homer 9, 20
house 22–23

L
language 20, 28, 34
logic 17

M
Mediterranean Sea 8–9
Minotaur 4, 29–33

Mount Olympus 18
myths 29–33

O
olives 6, 24
Olympic Games 19
oracle 18
ostrakon 15

P
Parthenon 10, 27
Peloponnesian War 11, 12–13
peplos 23
philosophy 16–17, 34, 45
Plato 17, 45
Ptolemy 16
Pythia 18

S
sacrifice 18, 35
sailing 6
science 16–17

slaves 14, 35, 44
Socrates 17, 45
soothsayer 18, 35
Sparta 4, 12, 13, 28
Spartan armies 12
sweetmeats 25
symposium 24, 35

T

temples 10, 18, 20, 27, 34, 44
theatres 20–21
Thebans 12

W

war 11, 12–13, 15, 19
weapons 11, 28
women 15, 22, 23, 44
writing 9, 20, 28, 34

www.two-canpublishing.com

Published by Two-Can Publishing
43–45 Dorset Street London W1U 7NA

© Two-Can Publishing 2001, 1998

For information on Two-Can books and multimedia,
call (0)20 7224 2440, fax (0)20 7224 7005, or visit our
website at http://www.two-canpublishing.com

Created by
act-two
346 Old Street
London EC1V 9RB

'Two-Can' is a trademark of Two-Can Publishing.
Two-Can Publishing is a division of Zenith Entertainment Ltd,
43–45 Dorset Street, London W1U 7NA.

ISBN 1–85434–927–9

2 4 6 8 10 9 7 5 3 1

A catalogue record for this book is available from the British Library

Photograph credits: AKG Photo: front cover;
Ancient Art and Architecture Collection: p.11 (r), p.14,
p.15 (b), p.20, p.23 (t); Bridgeman Art Library: p.26 (r),
p.27 (b); ET Archive: p.17, p.34 (l); Werner Forman:
pp.6–7; Michael Holford: p.11 (t,c), p.15 (t), p.19,
p.23 (b), p.24 (t), p.26 (l), p.27 (t), p.28, p.34 (tr), p.46,
p.47; Toby Maudsley: pp.25–25 (b), Zefa: p.34 (br).
Illustration credits: Mike Allport: pp.4–27, p.47, p.48;
Maxine Hamil: pp.29–33; Michele Egar, Carlo Tartaglia and
Jon Stuart: pp.8–9, pp.12–13, pp.44–45.

Every effort has been made to acknowledge correctly and
contact the source of each picture and Two-Can Publishing
apologises for any unintentional errors or omissions which
will be corrected in future editions of this book.

Printed in Hong Kong by Wing King Tong